Alexander Hamilton

First U.S. Secretary
of the Treasury

Colonial Leaders

Lord Baltimore *English Politician and Colonist*

Benjamin Banneker *American Mathematician and Astronomer*

William Bradford *Governor of Plymouth Colony*

Benjamin Franklin *American Statesman, Scientist, and Writer*

Anne Hutchinson *Religious Leader*

Cotton Mather *Author, Clergyman, and Scholar*

William Penn *Founder of Democracy*

John Smith *English Explorer and Colonist*

Miles Standish *Plymouth Colony Leader*

Peter Stuyvesant *Dutch Military Leader*

Revolutionary War Leaders

Benedict Arnold *Traitor to the Cause*

Nathan Hale *Revolutionary Hero*

Alexander Hamilton *First U.S. Secretary of the Treasury*

Patrick Henry *American Statesman and Speaker*

Thomas Jefferson *Author of the Declaration of Independence*

John Paul Jones *Father of the U.S. Navy*

Thomas Paine *Political Writer*

Paul Revere *American Patriot*

Betsy Ross *American Patriot*

George Washington *First U.S. President*

Alexander Hamilton

*First U.S. Secretary
of the Treasury*

Veda Boyd Jones

Arthur M. Schlesinger, jr.
Senior Consulting Editor

Chelsea House Publishers

Philadelphia

Produced by 21st Century Publishing and Communications, Inc.
New York, NY. http://www.21cpc.com

CHELSEA HOUSE PUBLISHERS
Editor in Chief Stephen Reginald
Production Manager Pamela Loos
Director of Photography Judy L. Hasday
Art Director Sara Davis
Managing Editor James D. Gallagher

Staff for *ALEXANDER HAMILTON*
Project Editor/Publishing Coordinator Jim McAvoy
Associate Art Director Takeshi Takahashi
Series Design Keith Trego

The Chelsea House World Wide Web address is
http://www.chelseahouse.com

First Printing
1 3 5 7 9 8 6 4 2

Library of Congress Cataloging-in-Publication Data

Jones, Veda Boyd.
Alexander Hamilton / by Veda Boyd Jones.
80 pp. cm. — (Revolutionary War Leaders series)
Includes bibliographical references and index.
Summary: Describes the career of Alexander Hamilton, who rose
from humble beginnings to become a delegate to the Constitutional
Convention and the first Secretary of the Treasury.
ISBN 0-7910-5354-7 (hc)   ISBN 0-7910-5697-X (pb)
1. Hamilton, Alexander, 1757-1804—Juvenile literature. 2. Statesmen—
United States—Biography—Juvenile literature. 3. United States—
Politics and government, 1783-1809—Juvenile literature. [1. Hamilton,
Alexander, 1757-1804. 2. Statesmen.] I. Title. II. Series.
E302.6.H2J66 1999
973.4'092—dc21   99-20695
[B]   CIP

Publisher's Note: In Colonial and Revolutionary War America, there were no standard rules for spelling, punctuation, capitalization, or grammar. Some of the quotations that appear in the Colonial Leaders and Revolutionary War Leaders series come from original documents and letters written during this time in history. Original quotations reflect writing inconsistencies of the period.

Contents

1 Life on the Islands   7

2 New Ideas   15

3 Fighting the Battles   29

4 Part of the "Family"   41

5 The New Nation   53

6 Politics to the End   65

Glossary   73

Chronology   74

Revolutionary War
Time Line   75

Further Reading   77

Index   78

Alexander spent most of his childhood on St. Croix, an island in the West Indies. The plantations on the island were a source of sugar for many countries all over the world. As a teenager, Alexander learned a lot about foreign trade while working in an import/ export business.

Life on
the Islands

Palm trees waved in the warm January sea breezes on the island of Nevis. In 1755 the British owned this tiny island in the West Indies. Here, on January 11, Alexander Hamilton was born.

Years earlier, when Alexander's mother was a teenager, she had married a much older man. They lived on the island of St. Croix and had a son named Peter. Alexander's mother was in a bad marriage and was unhappy. One day, she left her husband and son and moved to the island of Nevis.

There she met James Hamilton, the fourth son of a Scottish nobleman. He was also in an unhappy marriage. James had come to the West Indies to seek his fortune, but instead he went from job to job and never earned very much money.

Alexander's mother liked James and decided to move in with him. They lived together for many years and had two sons, James and Alexander. Alexander's parents were never married because his father was already married to another woman. This bothered Alexander because it was very unusual at that time.

Alexander had little schooling. His mother taught him at home. Her prize possessions were 34 books. Alexander read all of her books and had a good head for numbers.

When he was 10, his mother moved back to St. Croix and took her little family with her. This island was three times bigger than Nevis and was owned by Denmark. There were many sugar plantations on St. Croix. Of the 24,000 people who lived there, nearly 22,000 were slaves who worked in the sugarcane fields.

Alexander's family settled in the town of

Christiansted. When Alexander was 11 years old, his father left the family and moved to yet another island. To make money and support the family, his mother opened a small general store in their house. Still, they were very poor.

Because he was good in math, Alexander helped with the store's bookkeeping. He kept records of what supplies were in the storage house and how much each item cost. He even learned how to balance accounting books.

In February 1768 his mother became ill with a fever, and a few days later, so did Alexander. He got well, but his mother died. The two boys were left without any money and were treated as orphans. James, at 15, was **apprenticed** to a carpenter. Alexander, now 13, began work as a shipping clerk for an **import/export** business.

Alexander's boss, Nicholas Cruger, was from an old New York family. His shipping firm on St. Croix was only one of many locations for the large family shipping business. Ships brought in products from the British colonies in North

America. Cruger traded the lumber, livestock, and food that he imported for sugar from St. Croix. He also sent goods to other countries in Europe and South America.

Alexander had much to learn. He was already good with numbers from helping his mother do the bookkeeping. But his new job was much harder. He learned how to figure the rates of exchange from British, Spanish, and French money to Danish money. He also learned about foreign loans and interest payments.

Alexander was involved in world trade. He learned how much each ship could carry and where the good shipping lanes were. He was taught when to sell goods from the ships and when to wait for a better price.

The young man was good at his job, and he liked the work. But Alexander didn't like his lowly station in life. Around him were rich sugar plantation **aristocrats**. They owned land and slaves and lived lives of luxury. He wanted to be like them. But he wasn't like them. He had no

In the 1700s, New York was already a busy harbor where ships from many places, including St. Croix, unloaded and loaded their goods.

high-class family and no money. What he had was a lot of **ambition**. He wanted to be important.

Alexander wrote a letter to a friend about his dream of raising his station in life. He ended his letter by saying, "I wish there was a war." He dreamed of being a soldier. In battle he might win glory, fame, and power.

He also wrote poetry and sent a poem to a newspaper editor. The poem, about true love being twice as sweet for a married couple, was published. Alexander was proud when he saw his work in print.

In 1771 Nicholas Cruger went on a trip to New York. He left his 16-year-old clerk in charge of the shipping business. For the first time, Alexander felt powerful.

He had to make many decisions. He wrote to sea captains, government officials, and other merchants. He advised one captain to buy guns for his ship to fight off pirates. Alexander wrote letters to Cruger telling him about the business.

However, when Cruger returned, Alexander was again only a clerk and no longer in charge. He knew that he needed an education if he were to raise his place in life. He read all the books he could get his hands on. Then Alexander met Reverend Hugh Knox, who had recently come to St. Croix. The older man liked Alexander and tutored him, encouraging him to study hard.

In August 1772 a terrible hurricane hit the island. It pushed ships onto land and destroyed buildings. Saltwater rained on the sugarcane fields. Many people were killed or injured.

Alexander wrote about the violent hurricane. He described the fury of the wind and the roaring of the sea. Later, he showed his piece to Reverend Knox, who liked the writing and got the story published in the newspaper.

Many townspeople read the account of the hurricane and told the young man that it was good writing. Alexander had his second taste of local fame, and he liked it.

Reverend Knox spoke with Nicholas Cruger and other wealthy men on the island. He told them that Alexander was very smart and should go to college. The men agreed and put money in a fund to help pay for Alexander's schooling.

At the age of 17, Alexander had the chance he needed to change his life. He boarded a ship for North America and sailed away from the West Indies. He never returned.

New York Harbor around 1772. When Alexander arrived in New York to begin his new life, the city had 20,000 people. It was a very exciting place for someone who had lived on such a small island.

New Ideas

Anew life lay ahead for Alexander Hamilton. His adventure started before he landed on the North American shore. A fire broke out on his ship. Passengers helped sailors successfully fight the fire, and the ship sailed safely into harbor.

When Alexander first arrived in New York City, he met with friends of both Nicholas Cruger and Reverend Knox. He stayed a short while in the bustling city of 20,000 people. Unlike on the island, he saw no downtrodden slaves. Cheerful men and women walked downtown. Hundreds of stores lined the cobbled streets. Alexander liked the excitement of the city, but he had to leave it for the smaller town of Elizabethtown, New Jersey, to attend school there.

Because he had not gone to school before, Alexander needed to study basic subjects to prepare himself before he could go on to college. At Elizabethtown Academy he worked hard and learned math, public speaking, writing, and literature. He also studied Latin, Greek, and French.

He read many, many books. To remember what he read, he often copied sentences and then memorized them. Sometimes he walked in the graveyard next to the school, going over the information and talking to himself.

Alexander took letters of introduction from Reverend Knox to important people in town. His good manners and brilliant mind made him welcome in the homes of aristocrats Elias Boudinot and William Livingston. Alexander's family background was never talked about. And he never brought it up.

While visiting the homes of these men,

Alexander listened attentively to many interesting discussions. The main topic was the quarrel between the American colonists and Britain.

The British Parliament had passed new laws making the colonists pay more taxes. Boudinot and Livingston felt this was not right. Only the government of the **colony** should tax its own citizens. They elected the men in their own colony's legislature. They did not elect men in the British Parliament. If their own elected men passed laws they didn't like, they could vote them out of office. They could not vote anyone in the British Parliament out of office.

Both Boudinot and Livingston were on the colonists' side in the quarrel. They introduced Alexander to John Jay and other men who agreed with them.

Alexander had arrived in the American colonies as a loyal British subject, since he'd been born on a British island. But after hearing so much about taxation without representation, Alexander sided with the colonists. He thought

John Jay was a dedicated leader of the New York colonists. He also served in the Continental Congress.

the colonists should make their own laws. They should not be ruled by a far-off country.

Visiting with the Boudinot and Livingston

families was not all political. Alexander went on winter sleigh rides, a special treat since he was used to tropical weather. He learned to hunt and to enjoy sipping tea at cozy gatherings.

Alexander attended the Elizabethtown school as a special student. He moved through grade levels as fast as he could master the subjects. In only nine months he had learned enough to go to college. He planned to go to the College of New Jersey, the same school that Reverend Knox had gone to.

The president of that college would not let him enroll as a special student, however. He said Alexander had to go through the four-year program. Alexander was too impatient for that. Instead, he applied to King's College in New York City. This school let him learn at his own rate. In 1773 he moved to the bustling city.

Alexander's usual day at college started at five o'clock in the morning. Class work and studying kept him busy until eight o'clock at night. He studied math and science and read literature.

He kept up his habit of talking to himself to memorize important information.

King's College was run by men who strongly supported Britain. Alexander listened to their views but still agreed with the colonists. He saw America as the land of opportunity. Few people knew his family history, and this was a place where he could change his life.

During his first year at King's College, New Yorkers buzzed with talk of the Boston Tea Party. Alexander listened closely to the stories of the colonists refusing to pay a tax on tea. It was said that, in protest, the Bostonians had dumped shiploads of tea into the harbor. He felt he had to travel to Boston to find out what had happened.

On St. Croix Alexander had written about the hurricane. Now he wrote his opinion of the Boston Tea Party, which was published in a Boston newspaper. Back in New York, he showed the article to his friends. It was the first of many he wrote in defense of the colonists' rights to not pay British taxes.

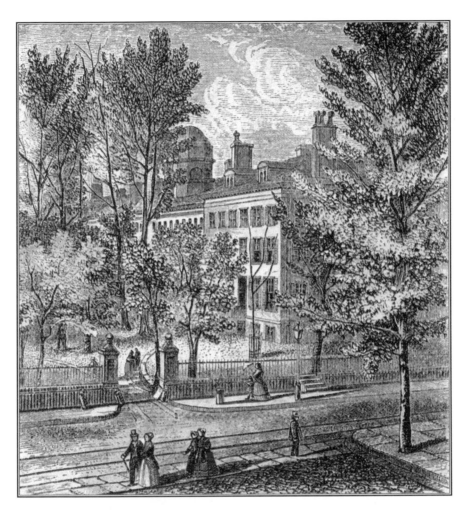

In 1773 Alexander enrolled in King's College in New York City. It later became Columbia College and is now Columbia University.

Of course, the English king was angry about the Boston Tea Party. He punished Boston by closing the harbor, so ships could not use it.

Angry colonists in Boston disguised themselves as Indians and dumped 10,000 pounds of British tea into Boston Harbor. This was known as the Boston Tea Party.

This outraged the colonists. Twelve of the 13 colonies sent **delegates** to Philadelphia, Pennsylvania, to meet and discuss how Britain was treating them. At this Continental Congress in

September 1774, the delegates voted not to buy goods from Britain or sell goods to Britain.

Many people in New York were against this idea, and in November a political **pamphlet** appeared. The author signed his name as A. W. Farmer. He wanted New York to keep trading with Britain. He said the farmers would be hurt very badly if they couldn't sell their crops to Britain and suggested that New Yorkers should disobey the Continental Congress.

Alexander read the pamphlet and disagreed. He wrote an answer to A. W. Farmer. His 35-page pamphlet said that most men wanted what was best for themselves. They put their needs above the good of others. Alexander believed all men in the colonies needed to stick together and make Britain do away with taxes. He wrote that Britain would be hurt if the colonists did not trade with them.

He signed his pamphlet as "A Friend of America." This time, in his hurry to respond, his writing was not very good. He repeated himself, and some of his facts were wrong. He knew he could do better, so he gathered pamphlets from other colonies and studied them.

Then A. W. Farmer wrote another pamphlet. This time, having done his homework well, Alexander was better prepared to answer A. W. Farmer. Alexander's second pamphlet was much better than his first one. It stuck to facts and made strong arguments in favor of the colonies. He wrote of the natural rights of man. He believed men should make laws for themselves and that men had a right to fight to overthrow any bad government.

When New Yorkers learned that "A Friend of America" was really a college student, they were quite surprised. Many thought the pamphlets had been written by very important men, like Alexander's older friends William Livingston or John Jay.

Alexander wrote many more essays that were published in the newspapers. He wanted the colonists to take a stand against Britain. If that meant a war, then so be it.

Other men also thought the colonists had a right to fight. In April 1775 shots were fired between British soldiers and the Massachusetts militia. The Continental Congress established an army and named George Washington as the commander. Alexander met George Washington when the great leader traveled through New York on his way to the fighting near Boston.

Alexander joined a volunteer group with other college students. Each morning he put on his green coat and his leather hat, on which was written "Liberty or Death." Alexander practiced marching and loading his musket and pretending to fire. Earlier in his life he had dreamed of a war, and now it was here. This could be his chance for honor.

Because he was good in math, Alexander decided to learn about **artillery**. He read about cannons and studied how far they could fire their cannonballs. He heard about a group of men who wanted to steal British cannons from the waterfront. The men met late on an August night. Out in the harbor sat a British warship. Could the men actually sneak aboard and take the cannons without being discovered?

Alexander desperately wanted to be part of the action. When he arrived at the waterfront, he found an older friend dragging a heavy cannon. Alexander handed his musket to his friend and took the ropes and pulled. The cannon wheels rumbled, and men's voices carried over the quiet bay.

Suddenly, British sailors saw the men. First, both sides exchanged musket shots. Then the British ship fired its huge guns.

Alexander quickly dragged the cannon to safety. He found his friend, who had dropped Alexander's musket when the fighting had started. Ignoring the danger, Alexander ran back to the waterfront and picked up his gun. He felt like he was a soldier, and he loved it.

When the war front moved from Boston toward New York, a call was made for more

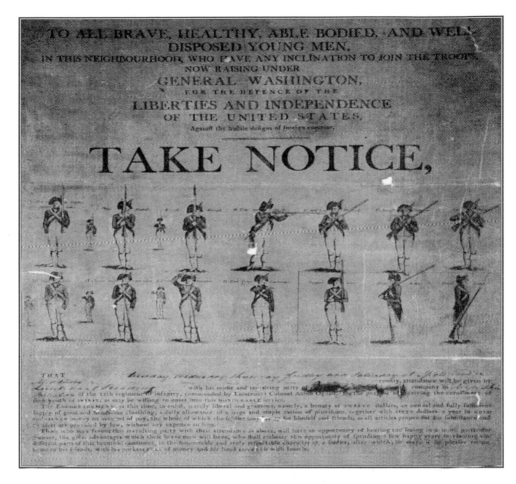

A recruitment poster for General George Washington's army. Alexander applied to be an artillery officer in the New York militia and was accepted.

soldiers. Alexander applied to be an artillery officer in the New York militia. His college studies were over. He became Captain Alexander Hamilton in March 1776. He was only 21.

Wearing the uniform of the New York artillery, Captain Hamilton was ready to fight the war. The young man from the West Indies without a high-class family background later became George Washington's most trusted aide.

3

Fighting the Battles

Captain Alexander Hamilton's New York artillery company looked shabby at its first drill. It sounded even worse. Alexander quickly found another drummer and a good **fife** player.

The cost of a uniform was to come out of each soldier's first paycheck. But Alexander wanted his troops to look special, so he paid part of the price of the uniforms for his men. This took the last of his school money from his West Indies friends.

Alexander ordered buckskinned trousers, deep blue coats with swallowtails and brass buttons, and three-cornered hats. He ordered special white pants for himself. He wanted to be a great soldier, and he wanted to look like one.

He drilled his men over and over. They learned to follow orders, march, and load cannons. His company of about 60 men was the sharpest-looking group in New York City.

When Alexander needed a lieutenant, he wanted to promote an enlisted man to the rank of officer. This had not been done before. Regular soldiers could not become officers. Usually a man's station in life, his family's social level, or his wealth decided if he could be an officer. This idea did not fit with Alexander's thinking. He had come from a poor, nontraditional family background. He felt that a person's ability and attitude should be rewarded. If a man was smart and honest, he should be a leader. Alexander talked New York lawmakers into letting the soldier become an officer.

It was time for Alexander's artillery company to get into the war. When Washington's army drove the enemy out of Boston, the British soldiers boarded ships and went to sea. Now Washington expected them to sail into New York harbor and launch an attack. At Fort George, which is at the tip of New York City, Alexander's men were ready and on the lookout for British ships.

On July 2 Alexander and his men watched as over 100 British ships sailed toward New York and anchored off Staten Island. But they did not come into the harbor and into cannon range. These were the same ships that had taken British soldiers out of Boston. Alexander heard from headquarters that the ships were waiting for more soldiers who were coming from Britain to join forces.

One week later a message came from General Washington's headquarters. It said the Continental Congress had declared the colonies free from Britain. The Declaration of Independence was read to Alexander's men. They cheered. Alexander was thrilled. He really had his war. And he was a part of the birth of a new nation.

Patriots cheer as the Declaration of Independence is read to the public for the first time on July 8, 1776. From then on they knew there could be no turning back.

Three days later his soldiers saw their first action. Around three o'clock in the afternoon, two warships sailed into New York Harbor and headed for the Hudson River. They passed directly by Alexander's command post. He gave the signal to fire all the cannons at once.

A huge roar filled the fort. Some men fell

dead. Others were wounded. The British ships had not fired at all as they sailed on by. Some of Alexander's cannons had burst, killing the men.

Alexander's first contact with the enemy was a terrible failure. The British ships had made it safely up the Hudson River. A rumor spread that Alexander hadn't trained his men properly. In truth, the cannonballs hadn't fit the old cannons. Alexander was upset and sad. That evening the dead men were buried.

Day after day more British ships arrived. They anchored in sight of the shore, but out of cannon reach. The sight terrified most New York citizens, who stayed in their homes. Alexander waited impatiently for something to happen.

One day a British officer was rowed ashore under a white flag of truce. He was blindfolded and taken to General Washington. Alexander knew the leaders would talk about peace. Would there be no war? Would his chance for glory be taken from him?

The British officer returned to his ship.

Alexander learned that the peace offering was for the Americans not to be put in jail. That was not enough. Americans wanted freedom. The war would continue!

On August 22 the British ships raised their sails. Instead of sailing toward Alexander's post, they sailed out of the harbor. A few days later, Alexander heard gunfire coming from Long Island. The British had landed there. Although Washington rushed troops to Long Island to fight, Alexander's company stayed on standby at Fort George.

The Battle of Long Island was a loss for the Americans. Word reached Alexander shortly before he heard gunfire close to New York City. Had his company been cut off by the British soldiers' advance up the East River?

By heading up the west side of the city, Alexander safely led his men to the American line. His troops, who had once dressed so sharply, now looked quite ragged. Many of his men needed new boots.

After losing the Battle of Long Island, American forces retreated to New Jersey. Here, in a show of force, British ships sail up the Hudson River to take Fort Lee, New Jersey.

His troops fell in with Washington's army and retreated from New York to New Jersey. With the enemy on their heels, they crossed the Raritan River at New Brunswick, New Jersey. American soldiers tore down half the bridge before the enemy arrived. Alexander's company set up cannons and fired at the enemy. They did no major damage, but they gave Washington's troops time to retreat. Alexander's men followed through the countryside, across the Delaware River, and into Pennsylvania.

Captain Hamilton fell ill. But when the call came on Christmas afternoon for a battle, he prepared to take part. Troops were given three days' worth of cooked food. They marched through the freezing wind toward the Delaware River.

No warming fires were allowed while they waited turns to board the ferry. The fires' glow might be seen by the enemy. Soon the howling wind blew heavy snow on the men. It was after midnight when Alexander's troops loaded their cannons on the icy ferry.

After crossing the Delaware, the troops marched eight miles to Trenton, New Jersey. Alexander's men set their cannons on one of the main streets. Through the blinding snow, Alexander caught sight of Hessian soldiers.

On Christmas night 1776, General Washington and his men face icy conditions as they cross the Delaware River. They then marched to attack the British at Trenton, New Jersey.

These were German soldiers hired by the British. Alexander gave the order to fire.

Many Hessians were killed. Some ran and

returned with two cannons while Alexander's men reloaded their cannons. Both sides fired. Cannonballs flew around Alexander, but he was not hit. More Hessians went down. Alexander's men reloaded and fired once more, and finally the Hessians surrendered.

The Americans knew that the British would rush troops to Trenton. Too tired for another battle, the Americans took their prisoners back to their Pennsylvania headquarters.

At the end of 1776, Alexander's men crossed the Delaware River again. Washington led them back to Trenton. British troops stormed across New Jersey and camped at one end of town. Instead of fighting there, Washington quietly moved his troops and left lighted campfires behind to fool the enemy. American troops then quickly swept around Trenton.

As British troops were marching out of Princeton, Washington's forces caught them by surprise and beat them badly. The British troops were scattered and ran away. A group of

British soldiers were holed up in a large brick building at the College of New Jersey. This was where Alexander had first planned to go to college. He carefully aimed his cannon at the building and fired.

The cannonball ripped through a window and hit a portrait of an earlier British king, George II, cutting his head off. Shortly afterward, stunned British soldiers filed out of the building and surrendered.

The fighting stopped while both armies went to their winter headquarters. The Continental Army took shelter in Morristown, New Jersey. Alexander made his way to Philadelphia. Here he received a letter from George Washington that was to mark the beginning of another great change in his life.

As General Washington's aide-de-camp, Alexander became part of the "family." His life centered around the general and his army. Here Washington reviews his troops during the bitterly cold winter of 1777–78 at headquarters in Valley Forge, Pennsylvania.

4

Part of the "Family"

General George Washington wanted young Alexander Hamilton as an **aide-de-camp**. Alexander thought seriously about the job.

If he took the job, it would raise his rank considerably, to lieutenant colonel. But he would be an assistant and would write letters for the general. He was unsure what other duties he would have. And if he took the job, he would not find glory on the battlefield. Fighting in a war and distinguishing himself had been his wish since his days working as a shipping clerk in the West Indies. He had seen that as the way to change his life.

Washington's other aides were from important, wealthy families. Several had been educated in Britain. Would Alexander fit in with them?

He respected General Washington and he thought that if he worked for him, perhaps he could talk the general into giving him a group of soldiers to command. Surely then he would become a war hero.

In March 1777 Alexander took the job and reported to headquarters for duty. His own New York artillery company became part of the Continental Army.

Alexander and General Washington were very different. At over six feet tall, the general towered over Alexander, who was only five feet seven inches tall. The general was also a big man, while Alexander was quite thin. The general had a kingly manner, listened carefully, and answered slowly. Alexander spoke with an eagerness that made his words pour out quickly.

Yet the two men were quite alike in a most important way. Washington said he wanted an aide-de-camp who could think as he did. Alexander could do this. He could write in the general's style and he could organize great amounts of information.

There were usually five or six aides-de-camp working at a time. They lived with the general at winter headquarters. The aides used one room of a local house for work and crowded into one room for sleeping. They called themselves the general's "family."

At winter headquarters, the general entertained important men. The aides-de-camp also attended these dinners. Here Alexander met many leaders from the Continental Congress.

Officers' wives also arrived at winter headquarters. They lived with their husbands until fighting began in the spring. They held gatherings and invited young women from the neighborhood. Alexander enjoyed the parties and was a favorite escort of the girls.

Alexander worked hard. He wrote letters to the Continental Congress and state leaders asking for more soldiers. Because he knew French, he also wrote to French leaders asking them to aid the new nation in the fight against Britain.

The other aides-de-camp took time off to be with their families. Since Alexander had no family in America and no land to care for, he stayed at winter headquarters with General Washington. Alexander was at the center of things. He saw how the new government operated. And he didn't like what he saw at all.

Officers of the Continental Army organized the Society of the Cincinnati. It was named after Cincinnatus, the Roman patriot who left his plow to fight for Rome. The society was limited to officers and their male descendants. The first president general was George Washington, and the second was Alexander Hamilton.

People in America considered themselves members of states. They referred to themselves as Virginians or New Yorkers. They did not think of themselves as Americans.

With no real ties to any state, Alexander saw himself as a man of the continent of America. He thought the states were too powerful and the

Continental Congress should be stronger. The Continental Congress could not tax people to get money for the war. Instead it had to ask the states for money. Some states gave more money than others to fight for freedom for all the states.

Alexander read many books about how other governments ran countries. He read about taxes, **finance**, and **economies**. He took notes in a logbook, so he wouldn't forget what he'd read. Then he wrote letters to state leaders saying the national government should be stronger.

General Washington trusted Alexander with important missions. He sent him to New York to get soldiers from another general. He asked Alexander to write a report on how to make the army stronger. He also sent Alexander to a meeting with British army officers to arrange an exchange of prisoners.

After the extremely harsh winter of 1777–78 at headquarters in Valley Forge, Pennsylvania, Alexander and many soldiers were discouraged. Some men deserted. But the news that the

French were sending troops to help cheered them up and they prepared for spring battles.

Usually Alexander was in the background of the battles. Sometimes he rode with General Washington to the battlefield to see how the troops were doing. In June 1778 at the Battle of Monmouth, he crisscrossed fields and woods, taking orders from the general to commanders. Daring as always, he rode to the front of the line. His horse was shot, and he fell injured, but he showed his courage.

Throughout the next year the American army held the enemy in New York. Alexander wrote more letters and continued reading and taking notes on government money matters. He was growing unhappy as an aide-de-camp. He wanted to command soldiers in battle.

During the winter of 1779–80, wives again joined their officer husbands and gave several parties. At one of these, Alexander met Elizabeth Schuyler, who was in the area visiting her aunt.

Elizabeth was an aristocrat. Her family was

wealthy and very important in New York. Her father had been a general in the war and a member of the Continental Congress. Elizabeth's privileged background was very different from Alexander's more humble beginnings.

The two young people fell in love. Although Alexander was ashamed of his family life in the West Indies, he told Elizabeth about his past. It didn't matter to her that he was not from a high-class family. The two wrote long letters to each other for nearly a year. Then, in December 1780, they were married.

A couple of months later at winter headquarters, General Washington told Alexander that he needed his help immediately. Alexander asked if he could first deliver a letter to one of the downstairs rooms on the first floor of the house and the general agreed.

Before he could return, Alexander met an officer in the hall and spoke with him for a minute or two. As Alexander hurried to climb the stairs, he saw the general standing at the top.

Elizabeth Schuyler was from a wealthy New York family. She and Alexander fell in love and were married in 1780.

General Washington began to scold Alexander for keeping him waiting for more than 10 minutes. Alexander knew it had not been that long, and he became angry at Washington. He resigned as the general's aide-de-camp. Later, the general sincerely apologized to Alexander, but Alexander would not take back his resignation.

He worked for General Washington for a few more months while they waited for a replacement. Then he went to Elizabeth's family's home in Albany, New York. Alexander started writing many letters to General Washington asking for a military command. He also wrote important newspaper essays about the need for a stronger government.

Artist Ralph Earle was in a debtors' prison in New York City. Alexander wanted him to paint a portrait of his wife. It was not proper for a lady to visit a prison, but Elizabeth Hamilton went anyway. Many people thought the portrait (at left) was wonderful. Other important ladies soon went to the prison to have their portraits painted. It wasn't long before the artist had earned enough money to be set free.

At last, in July 1781, General Washington gave Alexander command of a group of soldiers. Alexander would take part in the last great battle of the war at Yorktown, Virginia.

On October 14 Alexander led a bayonet

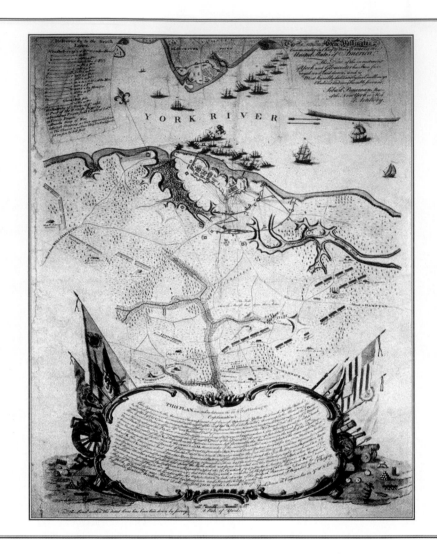

charge of 400 fighting men against a British **redoubt**, a small fort. He was the first one over the wall. His part of the battle lasted only 10 minutes, but it was successful. And it made Alexander feel like a war hero.

The plan of troop movements during the Battle of Yorktown, Virginia (left). During this last important battle of the Revolutionary War, Alexander successfully led a bayonet charge of 400 men against a British fort.

Three days later the British surrendered. America was free at last, and Alexander had finally fought in a war. Now, Alexander thought, it was time to help form and build the new nation.

George Washington takes the oath of office as the first president of the United States. Alexander Hamilton, the proud new secretary of the treasury, appears at far left with his hand in his vest.

The New Nation

With the war over, Alexander needed a job to support his wife and their infant son. He had liked reading law books while at school and decided to make a living as a lawyer.

Instead of the usual three years, he studied law for only three months before passing the New York law test. But in 1782, before he could open a law office, he was elected to the Continental Congress. As a congressman, Alexander saw how weak the national government was.

When he completed his term in the congress, he moved his family to New York City and set up a law office. Alexander truly understood the law. He was a brilliant lawyer and had many important clients.

He was very busy, but he still thought about the government. During the next few years, Alexander wrote many newspaper essays and pamphlets calling for a strong national government. He was still a gifted and speedy writer.

Alexander was chosen to represent New York City in the state legislature. He was also named a delegate to a meeting of all the states. The states' delegates were to discuss trade.

Only five states sent delegates to the meeting. That wasn't enough to make trade agreements. Besides, Alexander thought that what was really needed was a new central government—one with power to make laws about trade.

So Alexander wrote a letter calling for a constitutional convention. His words were too strong, so others at the trade meeting helped him reword his message. It called for another meeting of all states, this time to make changes necessary in the central government.

If it had not been for Shays's Rebellion, many states would not have sent delegates to the constitutional convention either. In the state of Massachusetts, some farmers, led by former Continental Army Captain Daniel Shays, attacked the courts. They wanted to stop farmers from being sent to **debtors**' prison. The Massachusetts governor asked for help from the Continental Congress, but it had no army to send. Other states saw the need for a stronger national government, so the states could get help when they needed it.

The Constitutional Convention was set for May 1787. Twelve states sent delegates, but one state—Rhode Island—did not. Alexander was one of three New York delegates. He listened carefully to speakers. On June 18 he rose to his feet and gave a five-hour speech, the longest of the convention.

He said the national government should be stronger than the states. He wanted a president elected for life. This sounded too much like a king to many of the delegates.

Alexander believed what he said in his speech, but he knew others would think it was extreme. That was part of his plan. If his ideas seemed too strong, perhaps the delegates would see the old government as too weak. They might **compromise** and decide on a plan that wasn't too strong or too weak.

Although the representatives decided on a plan different than the one Alexander wanted, he said he would support it. The new **Constitution** needed nine states to vote for it before it would be adopted.

To gain public support, the Constitution was printed in newspapers. Alexander asked John Jay and James Madison to help write essays about the Constitution. Each essay would explain a different section. There were a total of 85 essays published in New York newspapers. Alexander wrote more than 50 of them.

The 85 essays were later published in a book called *The Federalist.* It is still the best book about the American Constitution. It explained how the plan let individuals have rights, let states have power, and yet let the **federal**, or national, government join everyone together into one country.

To accept, or **ratify**, the Constitution, each state sent delegates to its own state convention. Most of New York's delegates were strongly against the Constitution. They met at the ratifying convention in June 1788. Hamilton led the fight for ratification. For every argument against the Constitution, he had an answer.

On June 24 news reached the New York delegates that New Hampshire had become the ninth state to ratify the Constitution. It was now the law of the land.

But what about the other states? What about the big states of Virginia and New York? Would they stay out of the new nation and make their own country?

On July 2 while the governor of New York was giving a speech against ratification, a rider galloped his horse to the meeting site with the news that Virginia had ratified the Constitution. The word spread quickly through the meeting that the biggest state had voted for ratification. Just three weeks later, the leader of the men against the Constitution said he would vote for it too. On the day he switched sides, a big parade was held in New York City, even before the final vote was taken.

The biggest float in the parade was a ship drawn by 10 horses and manned by 30 sailors. It was called the *Hamilton* after the man who had worked so hard for a strong new government.

Alexander Hamilton wasn't in New York City to see the parade. But his boss from the West Indies, Nicholas Cruger, watched it. The import/export businessman had known his young clerk would become an important leader. And he was right.

The Constitution passed in New York by three votes. New York became the 11th state in the nation. The other two states later ratified

A parade is held in New York to celebrate the upcoming ratification of the Constitution. The biggest float in the parade was a ship named *Hamilton*, for Alexander.

the plan. The Confederation of American States became the United States of America.

George Washington was elected the first president. He asked Alexander to be in charge of the United States Treasury Department. Alexander felt this would be the most powerful job in the new government, so he gave up his successful law practice and took the new job.

Congress ordered Alexander to draw up a financial plan. He wrote a long report. It said the United States should pay what it owed to foreign countries. It should pay off its debt to citizens. It should pay off the war debt of each state.

Congress knew the country should pay its bills, but congressmen argued about paying off state war debt. Some of the states owed more than others. Some had already paid their debt.

Another debate arose over where the capital of the country should be. Alexander made a deal with Thomas Jefferson, the secretary of state. Jefferson would help get the votes needed to pass the war debt act if Alexander would help get the votes needed to make the capital in the South. Both acts passed. The new capitol would be on land set aside from Virginia and Maryland and be named the District of Columbia.

Alexander's next big report was to set up a national bank. This caused a big rift between Jefferson and Alexander. Thomas Jefferson felt

Thomas Jefferson, secretary of state under President Washington. Later, Jefferson and Hamilton became leaders of opposing political parties.

that any power that was not in the Constitution was left to the states. Alexander felt that the Constitution called for the national government

The Bank of the United States, on Third Street in Philadelphia. Alexander successfully argued that a strong national bank was important to a sound government.

to take powers that were necessary to set up the government. Jefferson said starting a national bank wasn't in the Constitution. Alexander said it was absolutely necessary for a sound national government. Congress voted for the bank.

Which should be more powerful? State governments or the national government? This one argument between these two men started the two-party political system.

Alexander sent more reports to Congress. He wanted a national mint that printed money and made coins. He wrote a long-range manufacturing plan.

Some of the members of Congress raised questions about Alexander's honesty. He showed that his account books were in good order, but was upset by the lack of trust.

Alexander Hamilton's statue stands outside the U.S. Treasury Department Building in Washington, D.C. The sign on it reads, "First Secretary of the Treasury, Soldier, Orator, Statesman, Champion of Constitutional Union, Representative Government, and National Integrity."

Jefferson submitted his resignation as secretary of state in 1793. A little more than a year later, Alexander resigned as secretary of the treasury. Although they didn't hold government jobs upon resigning, both remained leaders of the new political parties.

In New York City in the early 1800s, people strolled down Broadway on Sunday afternoons. After he left the government, Alexander lived in New York until his death in 1804.

Politics to the End

After leaving the government, Alexander worked at his law office in New York City. He was an important member of the community. Each Sunday afternoon he and his family followed New York custom. They walked down Broadway and other main streets, talking to friends they met.

Alexander was a trusted advisor to the president. When Washington was ready to retire, he sent Alexander a copy of his farewell address and asked him to rewrite it. Alexander worked hard on it. He wrote that people should think of their country as one nation instead of many states.

Who would be the new president? The Constitution said the president had to be born in the United States or be a citizen when the country was formed. Alexander was a citizen, yet his party didn't pick him as their candidate.

His political party chose John Adams, who had been vice president when Washington was president. Alexander's party wanted Thomas Pinckney for vice president. The other party ran Thomas Jefferson for president and Aaron Burr for vice president.

In 1796 the top two vote-getters were elected. John Adams became president and Thomas Jefferson became vice president, even though they were from different parties.

Under President John Adams, relations with France were not very good. Many people thought there might be a war. Just in case, Congress voted to build up an army. President Adams asked George Washington to serve as commander-in-chief. Washington said he would only if Alexander Hamilton served as inspector

John Adams, second president of the United States. Jefferson was vice president under Adams, even though they were from different political parties.

general. That meant Alexander was in charge of organizing the new forces.

Alexander's old dream of achieving military

glory might come true after all. He spent two years building up an army. But President Adams kept the United States out of war with France, and the new army was disbanded. Alexander was disappointed.

President Adams did not like Alexander, and Alexander didn't like him. Before the 1800 election, Alexander told many people why Adams wasn't a good president. Alexander wanted Thomas Pinckney, his party's vice presidential nominee, to be president.

Once again, the other party ran Thomas Jefferson for president and Aaron Burr for vice president. This time the election was a tie between Jefferson and Burr. The House of Representatives had to break the tie.

Who would be the next president? Alexander had very different views than Jefferson. But Alexander hated Burr because he felt that Burr was not trustworthy. Alexander wrote letters asking congressmen not to vote for Burr. In one letter he wrote that Burr was "the most unfit man

Alexander in his job of inspector general of the army. Under President Adams, Alexander spent two years organizing a new army.

in the United States for the office of President."

Alexander was very relieved when Jefferson was elected president. At least Jefferson was an honest man. But he was not as happy that Aaron Burr was elected the next vice president.

Since Alexander's party was no longer in power, he knew his political influence was over. He worked at his law practice and founded the *New York Evening Post* newspaper.

In 1801 Alexander's son Philip was killed in a **duel**. A man had said bad things about Alexander's ideas, and Philip felt honor-bound to defend his father. After her brother Philip's death, one of Alexander's daughters went insane.

Alexander was filled with deep despair. To try to overcome his grief, he worked even harder at his law office.

Alexander still hated Aaron Burr. He was quoted in a newspaper as saying Burr was dangerous. Then Burr challenged him to a duel. Alexander thought dueling was wrong, but he didn't want people to think he was a coward. Being brave like a soldier was very important to him.

For two weeks he put his affairs in order. He wrote long letters of farewell to his friends and drew up a detailed will. He also wrote that he wasn't going to fire his gun. However, he didn't tell his wife about the duel.

Because New York had a law against duels, Alexander was rowed across the Hudson River to Weehawken, New Jersey, early on July 11, 1804. A friend, who served as his **second**, and a doctor were with him. Vice President Burr was already at the appointed spot with his second.

The rules of dueling were followed, with the seconds loading the guns and pacing off the 10 yards between Alexander and Burr. One of the seconds yelled, "Pre-SENT."

Both men raised their guns into the air. Burr fired, and his bullet hit Alexander in the stomach. Alexander's gun went off in reflex.

Alexander was carried to the rowboat and taken to a friend's home. His wife and seven children were sent for. Alexander died on the following day.

An outpouring of national grief followed Alexander Hamilton's unfortunate death. At a

Alexander's deadly duel with Aaron Burr. Before the duel Alexander had decided not to fire his gun. He was shot in the stomach and died the next day.

public funeral, he was remembered as a proud man who cared about the country. He had always spoken his views about building a strong nation. Alexander Hamilton had not tried to please the people. He had stood for what would help them.

GLOSSARY

aide-de-camp–a military assistant

ambition–a strong desire to do something important

apprentice–a person learning a trade from a skilled worker

aristocrat–a person in the upper class

artillery–large guns mounted on wheels

colony–land owned by a distant nation

compromise–to accept something that isn't exactly what you wanted

constitution–the law and plan of government

debtor–a person who owes something to another person

delegate–a person who represents others

duel–a fight with weapons between two people

economy–the way a country runs its trade and money

export–to send goods to another country to sell

federal–national

fife–a small flute-like musical instrument

finance–management of money

import–to bring in goods from another country

pamphlet–a small booklet

ratify–approve

redoubt–a small fort

second–an attendant of a person in a duel

CHRONOLOGY

1755	Born on January 11 on West Indian island of Nevis.
1768	Begins work as a shipping clerk for Nicholas Cruger.
1772	Arrives in North America for schooling.
1776	Appointed captain of New York artillery company.
1777	Appointed aide-de-camp to General George Washington.
1780	Marries Elizabeth Schuyler.
1781	Commands battalion at Battle of Yorktown.
1782	Becomes a lawyer; selected as delegate to the Continental Congress.
1787	Serves in New York State Assembly; is delegate to Constitutional Convention.
1787–88	Writes *Federalist* essays with James Madison and John Jay.
1789	Appointed secretary of the treasury by President George Washington.
1790	Feud begins with Thomas Jefferson that leads to formation of two political parties.
1795	Resigns as secretary of the treasury to return to law practice in New York.
1798	Appointed inspector general of the army.
1804	Dies on July 12, a day after being wounded by Aaron Burr in a duel.

REVOLUTIONARY WAR TIME LINE ===

1765   The Stamp Act is passed by the British. Violent protests against it break out in the colonies.

1766   Britain ends the Stamp Act.

1767   Britain passes a law that taxes glass, painter's lead, paper, and tea in the colonies.

1770   Five colonists are killed by British soldiers in the Boston Massacre.

1773   People are angry about the taxes on tea. They throw boxes of tea from ships in Boston harbor into the water. It ruins the tea. The event is called the Boston Tea Party.

1774   The British pass laws to punish Boston for the Boston Tea Party. They close Boston harbor. Leaders in the colonies meet to plan a response to these actions.

1775   The battles of Lexington and Concord begin the American Revolution.

1776   The Declaration of Independence is signed. France and Spain give money to help the Americans fight Britain. Nathan Hale is captured by the British. He is charged with being a spy and is executed.

1777   Leaders choose a flag for America. The American troops win some important battles over the British. General Washington and his troops spend a very cold, hungry winter in Valley Forge.

1778 France sends ships to help the Americans win the war. The British are forced to leave Philadelphia.

1779 French ships head back to France. The French support the Americans in other ways.

1780 Americans discover that Benedict Arnold is a traitor. He escapes to the British. Major battles take place in North and South Carolina.

1781 The British surrender at Yorktown.

1783 A peace treaty is signed in France. British troops leave New York.

1787 The U.S. Constitution is written. Delaware becomes the first state in the Union.

1789 George Washington becomes the first president. John Adams is vice president.

FURTHER READING

Egger-Bovet, Howard, and Marlene Smith-Baranzini. *U.S. Kids History: Book of the New American Nation.* Boston: Little, Brown & Co., 1995.

Fritz, Jean. *Shh! We're Writing the Constitution.* New York: Putnam Publishing Group, 1998.

Kallen, Stuart A. *Alexander Hamilton.* Minneapolis: ABDO Publishing, 1999.

Kent, Zachary. *The Surrender at Yorktown.* Danbury, CT: Children's Press, 1989.

Levy, Elizabeth. *If You Were There When They Signed the Constitution.* New York: Scholastic, 1992.

Mitchell, Carolyn B., et al. *BipQuiz: Revolutionary War.* New York: Sterling Publishing, 1996.

Penner, Lucille Recht. *The Liberty Tree: The Beginning of the American Revolution.* New York: Random House, 1998.

INDEX

Adams, John, 66, 68

Boston Tea Party, 20-21
Boudinot, Elias, 16-19
British Parliament, and taxation of
    colonies, 17-18, 20-25
Burr, Aaron, 66, 68-69, 70-72

Constitution
    and Hamilton, 54-58, 61-62
    president in, 66
    ratification of, 56-59
Constitutional Convention, 54-56
Continental Congress, 23-24, 25, 31,
    43-44, 45, 47, 53, 55
Cruger, Nicholas, 9-10, 12, 13, 15, 58

Declaration of Independence, 31
District of Columbia, 60

Elizabethtown Academy, 16, 19

Farmer, A. W., 23, 24
Federalist, The, 56-57

Hamilton (parade float), 58
Hamilton, Alexander
    as aide-de-camp to Washington,
        41-49
    birth of, 7
    as captain of New York artillery
        company, 29-39
    childhood of, 7-13
    children of, 53, 70, 71
    as commander in Battle of
        Yorktown, 49-51
    and Constitution, 54-58, 61-62
    in Continental Congress, 53
    death of from duel with Burr, 70-
        72
    education of, 8, 9, 12, 13, 16, 19-20,
        25-26, 27

    family of, 7-9, 16
    father of, 7-8, 9
    as inspector general of army, 66-
        68
    and Jefferson, 60-63
    as lawyer, 53-54, 59-60, 65, 70
    mother of, 7-8, 9
    and national bank, 60-62
    and national mint, 63
    in New York State Assembly, 54
    and Revolutionary War, 25-51
    as secretary of the treasury, 59-63
    as shipping clerk, 9-11, 12, 41
    and taxation by British Parliament,
        17-18, 20-25
    and views on government, 44-45,
        54, 55-56, 60-63, 65, 72
    in West Indies, 7-13
    wife of, 46-47, 49, 53, 71
    writings of, 12, 13, 20, 23-25, 49,
        54, 56-57
Hamilton, Elizabeth Schuyler (wife),
    46-47, 49, 53
Hamilton, James (brother), 8, 9
Hamilton, James (father), 7-8, 9
Hamilton, Philip (son), 70
Hessian soldiers, 36-38
House of Representatives, 68

Jay, John, 17, 24, 56
Jefferson, Thomas, 60-63, 66, 68, 69

King's College, 19-20
Knox, Hugh, 12, 13, 15, 16, 19

Livingston, William, 16-19, 24
Long Island, Battle of, 34

Madison, James, 56
Monmouth, Battle of, 46

New York Evening Post, 70

Pinckney, Thomas, 66, 68
Political parties, 63, 66, 68

Revolutionary War, 25-51

Shay's Rebellion, 55

Trenton, Battle of, 36-38

Valley Forge, Pennsylvania, 45-46

Washington, George, 59, 66
   as commander-in-chief under
      Adams, 66
   farewell address of, 65
   Hamilton as aide-de-camp to,
      41-49
   and Revolutionary War, 25, 30,
      31, 33, 35, 38, 39

Yorktown, Battle of, 49-51

PICTURE CREDITS

page

3: The Library of Congress
6: Stokes Collection/Prints Division/
   The New York Public Library
11: Stokes Collection/Prints Division/
   The New York Public Library
14: Stokes Collection/Prints Division/
   The New York Public Library
18: The Library of Congress
21: Stokes Collection/Prints Division/
   The New York Public Library
22: The Library of Congress
27: The Library of Congress
28: Picture Collection/The New York
   Public Library
32: National Archives
35: U.S. Naval Academy Museum
37: National Archives

40: The Library of Congress
48: National Archives
50: Stokes Collection/Prints Division/
   The New York Public Library
51: National Archives
52: The Library of Congress
59: The Library of Congress
61: The Library of Congress
62: Stokes Collection/Prints Division/
   The New York Public Library
64: Stokes Collection/Prints Division/
   The New York Public Library
67: National Archives
69: Stokes Collection/Prints Division/
   The New York Public Library
72: Picture Collection/The New York
   Public Library

ABOUT THE AUTHOR

Award-winning writer **VEDA BOYD JONES** enjoys the challenge of writing for a variety of readers. Her published works include nine adult novels, four children's historical novels, six children's biographies, a coloring book, and numerous articles and short stories in national magazines. In addition to working at her computer, she teaches writing and speaks at writers' conferences. Mrs. Jones lives in the Missouri Ozarks with her husband, Jimmie, and three sons, Landon, Morgan, and Marshall.

Senior Consulting Editor **ARTHUR M. SCHLESINGER, JR.** is the leading American historian of our time. He won the Pulitzer Prize for his book *The Age of Jackson* (1945), and again for *A Thousand Days* (1965). This chronicle of the Kennedy Administration also won a National Book Award. He has written many other books, including a multi-volume series, *The Age of Roosevelt.* Professor Schlesinger is the Albert Schweitzer Professor of the Humanities at the City University of New York, and has been involved in several other Chelsea House projects, including the Colonial Leaders series of biographies on the most prominent figures of early American history.